ABUNDANT TRUTH INTERNATIONAL MINISTRIES

Abundant Truth Spiritual Gifts Series

DREAMS AND VISIONS

A Biblical Approach to Understanding Dreams and Visions

Roderick Levi Evans

Published by Abundant Truth Publishing

P.O. Box 126
Camden, NC 27921
Web: www.abundantpublishing.net
Email: abundantpublishing@gmail.com

Printed U.S.A.

Front & Back Cover Designs by Abundant Truth Publishing
All rights reserved.
Free-use Cover Image

Abundant Truth Publishing is a ministry of **Abundant Truth International Ministries.** The primary mission of ATI Ministries is to equip the Body of Christ with tools necessary to defend and contend for the truth of the Christian faith. Jesus Christ came to bear witness of the truth and ATI Ministries is a modern-day extension of His commission (John 18:37).

Abundant Truth Spiritual Gifts Series – Dreams and Visions
©2011 Abundant Truth Publishing
All Rights Reserved
ISBN13: 9781601412966

Unless otherwise indicated, all of the scripture quotations are taken from the *Authorized King James Version* of the Bible. Scripture quotations marked with NIV are taken from the *New International Version* of the Bible. Scripture quotations marked with NASV are taken from the *New American Standard Version* of the Bible. Scripture quotations marked with Amplified are taken from the *Amplified Bible*

Printed in the United States of America

Contents

Introduction

Chapter 1 – Dreams and Visions in the Old Testament   1

Establish Covenant and Purpose   5

Warn of Future Events   8

Encourage His Servants   12

Chapter 2 – Dreams and Visions in the New Testament   19

Foretell Future Events   21

Encourage His Servant   24

Provide Instruction and Direction   26

Contents *(cont.)*

Chapter 3 – Types of Dreams   35

Prophetic Dreams   *37*

State of the Union Dreams   *48*

Conditional Dreams   *55*

Chapter 4 – Types of Visions   65

Open Visions   *68*

Trances   *75*

Inner Visions   *81*

Night Visions   *88*

Chapter 5 – Other Types of Dreams and Visions   99

Personal Dreams   *101*

Contents *(cont.)*

Demonic Dreams — 107

False Visions — 110

Closing Thoughts on Understanding Dreams and Visions — 117

Introduction

The promise of the Father was the fulfillment of God's prophecy through Joel. One result of the Spirit's coming would be prophetic revelation and the manifestation of dreams and visions. We discover from Paul's discussions of the gifts in I Corinthian 12 that the Spirit is responsible for the dispersion of the gifts. In the Abundant Truth Spiritual Gifts Series, we will examine the gifts of the Spirit and their operations in the New Testament Church.

In this publication:

This publication presents a solid foundation for the plan, purpose, and operation of dreams and visions. When Jesus made us citizens of the Kingdom, it came with advantages. As members of the kingdom of God, we are eligible to partake of the outpouring of the Spirit.

When Jesus made us citizens of the Kingdom, it came with advantages. As members of the kingdom of God, we are eligible to partake of the outpouring of the Spirit. The books of Joel and the Acts declare that the direct result of the outpouring of the Spirit of God would be revelation. Men and women could receive and communicate by the Spirit of God; two ways this is done is through **dreams and visions**.

> *And it shall come to pass afterward, that I will pour out my spirit upon all flesh; and your sons and your daughters shall prophesy, your old men shall dream dreams, your young men shall see visions. (Joel 2: 28)*
>
> *But this is that which was spoken by the prophet Joel; And it shall come to pass in the last days, saith God, I will*

pour out of my Spirit upon all flesh: and your sons and your daughters shall prophesy, and your young men shall see visions, and your old men shall dream dreams. (Acts 2:16, 17)

In the first book of this two-part series, we will discuss the differing manifestations of dreams and visions. We will also explore the varying types and their role in the Christian life.

DREAMS AND VISIONS

- Chapter 1 -
Dreams and Visions in the Old Testament

DREAMS AND VISIONS

DREAMS AND VISIONS

Dreams and visions are historical vehicles for the revelation of God. God would impart knowledge of future events and impending dangers to His people through visions.

In this chapter, we will discuss the biblical history of dreams and visions among the Old Testament patriarchs and prophets. We will discover that dreams and visions are a common occurrence among the people of the Lord. We can also benefit from them today.

The Old Testament is full of examples of God using dreams and visions. The first

DREAMS AND VISIONS

biblical record of God using a dream for communication is found in the twentieth chapter of Genesis. Abraham had instructed Sarah to tell men wherever they traveled that they were siblings rather than husband and wife.

As a result, in the land of the Gerar, king Abimelech, who planned to take her as his own,
brought her to his place. However, God appeared to him in a dream,

> But God came to Abimelech in a dream by night, and said to him, Behold, thou art but a dead man, for

DREAMS AND VISIONS

the woman which thou hast taken; for she is a man's wife. (Genesis 20:3)

This first recorded dream would mark the beginning of a legacy of God speaking to men in dreams and visions. In the Old Testament God used dreams and visions for various reasons. To understand their roles in the lives of Christians, we will consider a few biblical records. Dreams and visions came from God to:

Establish Covenant & Purpose

God used dreams to reveal His purpose. Dreams and visions were given to bring men into a greater understanding of

DREAMS AND VISIONS

God and His activities in the earth. His primary modes of communication to His people were dreams and visions.

> *And he said, Hear now my words: If there be a prophet among you, I the Lord will make myself known unto him in a vision, and will speak unto him in a dream. (Numbers 12:6)*

In addition, God used dreams to establish covenant and relationship with His Servants. God established His covenant with Abraham and his descendants through dreams and visions. He revealed to them what He would do for them if they walk

DREAMS AND VISIONS

before Him in righteousness. Consider Abraham:

After these things the word of the Lord came unto Abram in a vision, saying, Fear not, Abram: I am thy shield, and thy exceeding great reward. (Genesis 15:1).
Consider Jacob:

And Jacob went out from Beersheba, and went toward Haran. And he dreamed, and behold a ladder set up on the earth, and the top of it reached to heaven: and behold the angels of God ascending and descending on it. And, behold, the Lord stood above it, and said, I am the Lord God of Abraham thy father, and the God of Isaac: the land whereon thou liest, to thee will I give it, and to thy seed. (Genesis 28:10, 12-13)

Warn of Future Events

God sent dreams and visions in the Old Testament to warn His servants of impending danger. Dreams and visions provided warning and protection to the servants of the Lord. When they faced dangers or even God's judgment, God would warn them through these modes of revelation.

DREAMS AND VISIONS

Behold, thou art but a dead man, for the woman which thou hast taken... (Genesis 20:3)

This is what the Lord did for Abimelech from our opening scripture. God appeared to the king in a dream warning him to restore Sarah to Abraham or there would be consequences. Dreams and visions were used to foretell future world and natural events.

God used dreams to reveal future famines and kingdoms. These were done to establish His sovereignty over all the earth. He revealed to Pharaoh the famine that was

DREAMS AND VISIONS

to come upon the earth.

And Joseph said unto Pharaoh, The dream of Pharaoh is one: God hath shewed Pharaoh what he is about to do. Behold, there come seven years of great plenty throughout all the land of Egypt: And there shall arise after them seven years of famine; and all the plenty shall be forgotten in the land of Egypt; and the famine shall consume the land; And the plenty shall not be known in the land by reason of that famine following; for it shall be very grievous. And for that

DREAMS AND VISIONS

the dream was doubled unto Pharaoh twice; it is because the thing is established by God, and God will shortly bring it to pass (Genesis 41:25, 29-32).

He also revealed to Nebuchadnezzar the future of his kingdom.

But there is a God in heaven that revealeth secrets, and maketh known to the king Nebuchadnezzar what shall be in the latter days. Thy dream, and the visions of thy head upon thy bed, are these; As for thee, O king, thy thoughts came into thy mind upon

DREAMS AND VISIONS

thy bed, what should come to pass hereafter: and he that revealeth secrets maketh known to thee what shall come to pass (Daniel 2:28-29).

Encourage His Servants

God also used dreams and visions to encourage His servants concerning future ministries. God revealed to Joseph his future ministry and leadership through dreams. He had these dreams approximately thirteen years before their fulfillment.

And he said unto them, Hear, I pray you, this dream which I have

DREAMS AND VISIONS

dreamed: For, Behold, we were binding sheaves in the field, and, lo, my sheaf arose, and also stood upright; and, behold, your sheaves stood round about, and made obeisance to my sheaf. He dreamed yet another dream, and told it his brethren, and said, Behold, I have dreamed a dream more; and, behold, the sun and the moon and the eleven stars made obeisance to me. (Genesis 37:6, 7, 9)

God also used dreams and visions to encourage His servants in difficult times.

DREAMS AND VISIONS

God used dreams and visions to encourage His servants. He gave Jacob a dream to comfort him during his stay with Laban.

> *And it came to pass at the time that the cattle conceived, that I lifted up mine eyes, and saw in a dream, and, behold, the rams which leaped upon the cattle were ringstraked, speckled, and grisled. And the angel of God spake unto me in a dream, saying, Jacob: And I said, Here am I. And he said, Lift up now thine eyes, and see, all the rams which leap upon the cattle are ringstraked, speckled, and*

DREAMS AND VISIONS

grisled: for I have seen all that Laban doeth unto thee.(Genesis 31:10-12).

God also gave Gideon's enemies a dream that encouraged him to go to battle.

And when Gideon was come, behold, there was a man that told a dream unto his fellow, and said, Behold, I dreamed a dream, and, lo, a cake of barley bread tumbled into the host of Midian, and came unto a tent, and smote it that it fell, and overturned it, that the tent lay along. And his fellow answered and said, This is nothing

DREAMS AND VISIONS

else save the sword of Gideon the son of Joash, a man of Israel: for into his hand hath God delivered Midian, and all the host. (Judges 7:13-14)

Dreams and visions were a common occurrence since the beginning. They served many purposes. The Bible is full of accounts of dreams and visions (not mentioned above). They were and still are an important part of God's communication to His people. With the establishment of the New Covenant, dreams and visions still proved to be a valuable resource to receive revelation from God.

DREAMS AND VISIONS

Notes:

DREAMS AND VISIONS

-Chapter 2-
Dreams and Visions in the New Testament

DREAMS AND VISIONS

DREAMS AND VISIONS

Dreams and visions continued into the New Testament and after the birth of the Church. God granted the m as He deemed necessary. They proved to be effective means of communication. Here are some New Testament records of the manifestation of dreams and visions.

Foretell Future Events

God gave Joseph and Mary dreams and visions to foretell and announce Jesus' birth. He allowed the angel Gabriel to appear to them in dreams and visions to give them instructions concerning the Christ.

DREAMS AND VISIONS

But while he thought on these things, behold, the angel of the Lord appeared unto him in a dream, saying, Joseph, thou son of David, fear not to take unto thee Mary thy wife: for that which is conceived in her is of the Holy Ghost. And she shall bring forth a son, and thou shalt call his name JESUS: for he shall save his people from their sins. (Matthew 1:20-21)

And the angel came in unto her, and said, Hail, thou that art highly favoured, the Lord is with thee: blessed art thou among women. And

DREAMS AND VISIONS

when she saw him, she was troubled at his saying, and cast in her mind what manner of salutation this should be. And the angel said unto her, Fear not, Mary: for thou hast found favour with God. And, behold, thou shalt conceive in thy womb, and bring forth a son, and shalt call his name Jesus. (Luke 1:28-31)

While in exile on the island of Patmos, God foretold the future end of all things to John through visions.

Who bare record of the word of God, and of the testimony of Jesus Christ,

DREAMS AND VISIONS

and of all things that he SAW. (Revelation 1:2, Emphasis Mine)

Encourage His Servants

Dreams and visions were used by encourage servants of Christ. Stephen had a vision of Christ at his stoning. Stephen was allowed to see the heavens opened. He saw Christ standing at the right of God.

But he, being full of the Holy Ghost, looked up steadfastly into heaven, and saw the glory of God, and Jesus standing on the right hand of God. (Acts 7:55)

DREAMS AND VISIONS

This vision provided encouragement and comfort to Stephen who would become one the Church's first martyrs.

Cornelius had a vision of Gabriel encouraging him that God had heard his prayers and received his good works. Cornelius received a vision from God instructing him to send for Peter. God allowed his eyes to perceive the angel of the Lord speaking to him.

> *He saw in a vision evidently about the ninth hour of the day an angel of God coming in to him, and saying unto him, Cornelius. And when he looked*

DREAMS AND VISIONS

on him, he was afraid, and said, What is it, Lord? And he said unto him, Thy prayers and thine alms are come up for a memorial before God. (Acts 10:3-4)

Provide Instruction and Direction

The apostles had a vision of the angel of the Lord who gave them directions for ministry. After being thrown in prison, the apostles saw the angel of the Lord who gave them instructions on where to preach next.

But the angel of the Lord by night opened the prison doors, and

DREAMS AND VISIONS

brought them forth, and said, Go, stand and speak in the temple to the people all the words of this life. (Acts 5:19-20)

Peter had a vision on the rooftop instructing Him concerning God's plan to receive the Gentiles into the faith. God gave Peter a vision (through a trance) while he was waiting to eat. This would herald the entrance of the Gentiles into the Christian faith.

And he became very hungry, and would have eaten: but while they made ready, he fell into a trance, And

DREAMS AND VISIONS

saw heaven opened, and a certain vessel descending unto him, as it had been a great sheet knit at the four corners, and let down to the earth: Wherein were all manner of fourfooted beasts of the earth, and wild beasts, and creeping things, and fowls of the air. And there came a voice to him, Rise, Peter; kill, and eat. (Acts 10:10-13)

Paul received a vision directing him to go to Macedonia. While traveling and ministering, Paul received a vision, which demanded his entrance into Macedonia

DREAMS AND VISIONS

with the Gospel.

And a vision appeared to Paul in the night; There stood a man of Macedonia, and prayed him, saying, Come over into Macedonia, and help us. And after he had seen the vision, immediately we endeavored to go into Macedonia, assuredly gathering that the Lord had called us for to preach the gospel unto them. (Acts 16:9-10)

It is understood that in both Covenants God used dreams and visions to communicate to His people. Dreams and

DREAMS AND VISIONS

visions are still valuable to the Church today. One of the direct results of the Spirit's outpouring would be dreams and visions.

But this is that which was spoken by the prophet Joel; And it shall come to pass in the last days, saith God, I will pour out of my Spirit upon all flesh: and your sons and your daughters shall prophesy, and your young men shall see visions, and your old men shall dream dreams. (Acts 2:16, 17)

As we continue our study, we endeavor to impart an appreciation and

DREAMS AND VISIONS

understanding of dreams and visions in the Body of Christ today.

DREAMS AND VISIONS

DREAMS AND VISIONS

Notes:

_____

_____

_____

_____

_____

_____

_____

_____

_____

_____

DREAMS AND VISIONS

-Chapter 3-
Types of Dreams

DREAMS AND VISIONS

DREAMS AND VISIONS

Dreams are powerful vehicles of revelation and insight. They can change the course of an individual's life because of their impact. Dreams come to fulfill different purposes. Therefore, dreams come as responses to the different circumstances in our lives.

In this chapter, we will examine the different types of dreams and their sources. To begin our examination of dreams, we will look at prophetic dreams.

Prophetic Dreams

The prophetic dream comes to reveal a message from the Lord. The

DREAMS AND VISIONS

prophetic dream serves the same purpose as a prophetic word. The scriptures tell us that when one prophesies, he speaks unto edification, exhortation, and comfort.

> *But he that prophesieth speaketh unto men to edification, and exhortation, and comfort. (I Corinthians 14:3)*

The prophetic dream is the spirit of prophecy being expressed through images. These types of dreams will draw an individual closer to the Lord. The prophetic dream is the voice of the Lord through visualization. The prophetic dream will

DREAMS AND VISIONS

edify, exhort, and comfort the receiver. In addition, they will give us instructions from the Lord and show us things that are to come.

Edify

The prophetic dream comes to strengthen believers in their walks with the Lord. These dreams come to help us remain focused on our present course. They come to give us the necessary strength to make it through.

> *And the angel of God spoke unto me in a dream, saying, Jacob: and I said, Here am I. And he said, Lift up now*

DREAMS AND VISIONS

thine eyes, and see, all the rams which leap upon the cattle are ringstraked, speckled, and grisled: for I have seen all that Laban doeth unto thee. (Genesis 31:11-12)

Laban treated Jacob unfairly. Jacob watched over his cattle. Laban would promise him which cattle he could have as pay. However, if the promised cattle produced a great number, Laban would switch the cattle that Jacob could have.

Therefore, the Lord strengthened Jacob during his stay with Laban in dreams. The dreams showed him that no matter

DREAMS AND VISIONS

which cattle Laban chose to give him, they will produce many (Genesis 31:1-13).

Exhort

Prophetic dreams come also to exhort us to take some type of action. Prophetic dreams will direct us to continue to operate in righteousness. They will come to order our steps. Prophetic dreams of this sort will challenge you in how you handle people and situations.

And God came to Laban the Syrian in a dream by night, and said unto him, Take heed that thou speak not

DREAMS AND VISIONS

to Jacob either good or bad. (Genesis 31:24)

In the story of Laban and Jacob, we discover that many unfortunate events took place between them. Therefore, Jacob decided to leave without Laban's prior knowledge. God spoke to Laban and told (exhorted) him not to do anything to Jacob.

Comfort

The prophetic dream comes also to comfort us. God will send comfort and consolation to us in difficult circumstances and situations. There are numerous examples of this in the scripture.

DREAMS AND VISIONS

And when Gideon was come, behold, there was a man that told a dream unto his fellow, and said, Behold, I dreamed a dream, and, lo, a cake of barley bread tumbled into the host of Midian, and came unto a tent, and smote it that it fell, and overturned it, that the tent lay along. And his fellow answered and said, This is nothing else save the sword of Gideon the son of Joash, a man of Israel: for into his hand hath God delivered Midian, and all the host. And it was so, when Gideon heard the telling of the dream,

DREAMS AND VISIONS

and the interpretation thereof, that he worshipped... (Judges 7:13-15)

God gave Gideon's enemy a dream. The dream and the interpretation came to offer comfort to Gideon who was about to face battle. This is what the Lord does for us. He gives us dreams to remind us of His presence in our lives and to soothe our doubts and fears.

Direction/Instruction

The most common manifestation of the prophetic dream is one of direction and instruction from the Lord. The Lord gives these dreams to show us which path

DREAMS AND VISIONS

we are to take. When a prophetic dream of this nature is given, it appears in different forms. In the dream, you may see yourself doing or saying that which the Lord is instructing you to do or someone in the dream (individual, a voice, or an angel, etc.) may tell you what to do.

And when they were departed, behold, the angel of the Lord appeareth to Joseph in a dream, saying, Arise, and take the young child and his mother, and flee into Egypt, and be thou there until I bring thee word: for Herod will seek the

DREAMS AND VISIONS

young child to destroy him. (Matthew 2:13)

God gave Joseph divine direction in this dream. Though he was dreaming, an angel appeared to him in the dream to direct him.

Foretell & Reveal Future Events

Another common manifestation of the prophetic dream is those that reveal future events. The Lord gives these dreams because He delights in revealing things to His children. Though conditional dreams (discussed later in this chapter) reveal future events, they are based on certain

DREAMS AND VISIONS

events and circumstances in order to be fulfilled.

However, the prophetic dream reveals future events that are decreed from the Lord. These dreams will come to pass because they usually reveal God's perfect plan and purpose, which cannot be altered.

> *But there is a God in heaven that revealeth secrets, and maketh known to the king Nebuchadnezzar what shall be in the latter days. Thy dream, and the visions of thy head upon thy bed, are these; As for thee, O king, thy*

DREAMS AND VISIONS

thoughts came into thy mind upon thy bed, what should come to pass hereafter: and he that revealeth secrets maketh known to thee what shall come to pass. (Daniel 2:28-29)

Nebuchadnezzar's dream of the great image was given to him by God. The Lord revealed to him things that were going to happen. No condition or circumstance could change what he had seen.

State of the Union Dreams

In America, when the president comes forward to address the nation, it is

DREAMS AND VISIONS

called a "State of the Union" address. The purpose of such a speech is to notify the country of its present situation or condition, while also proposing future actions that should be taken. "State of the Union" dreams function in a similar manner.

These dreams help bring clarity to present circumstances or conditions, reveal personal thoughts and intents, expose spiritual warfare, as well as the intents and plans of others. We will now examine these aspects of the "State of the Union" dreams more closely.

DREAMS AND VISIONS

Clarify Conditions and Circumstances

In life, we experience difficult situations for which we have no understanding. Therefore, the Lord will give us dreams to clarify what we are experiencing. Joseph received this type of dream while wondering what he was to do with Mary, whom he discovered was pregnant.

But while he thought on these things, behold, the angel of the Lord appeared unto him in a dream, saying, Joseph, thou son of David, fear not to take unto thee Mary thy wife: for that

DREAMS AND VISIONS

which is conceived in her is of the Holy Ghost. And she shall bring forth a son, and thou shalt call his name JESUS: for he shall save his people from their sins. (Matthew 1:20-21)

When Joseph discovered that Mary was pregnant, he was faced with a hard decision. However, the Lord sent His word to him in a dream to strengthen him in the present circumstances.

Reveal Personal Thoughts and Intents

The scriptures declare that the heart is deceitful above all and desperately wicked.

DREAMS AND VISIONS

This implies that one can be vulnerable to self-deception. This type of dream comes to challenge us to face what is in our hearts and minds. In addition, it may reveal to us things we are planning to do.

Have you ever dreamt about saying something to someone that you would never dare to? Have you done certain things in dreams (good or bad) that you believe you would not do under normal circumstances?

The "State of the Union" dream comes to show us the hidden things in our hearts that we are not willing to face. This is to

DREAMS AND VISIONS

safeguard our future actions and inner motives. When God appeared to Abimelech after he had taken Sarah into his house, the Lord gave Him this type of dream along with a warning.

> *But God came to Abimelech in a dream by night, and said to him, Behold, thou art but a dead man, for the woman which thou hast taken; for she is a man's wife. But Abimelech had not come near her: and he said, Lord, wilt thou slay also a righteous nation? Said he not unto me, She is my sister? and she, even she herself*

said, He is my brother: in the integrity of my heart and innocency of my hands have I done this. (Genesis 20:3-5)

Abimelech intended to take Sarah as his wife. In addition, God informed him that He had been lied to and the woman was married. He warned Abimelech of impending punishment if he carried out the intent of his heart. The State of the Union dream does this in our lives. It causes us to face what is on the inside and provide warning against future unrighteous acts.

DREAMS AND VISIONS

Conditional Dreams

One of the difficult dreams to apply is the conditional dream. These types of dreams come to show us a potential outcome. The dream's fulfillment will or will not take place except certain events take place. However, when these dreams come, they come as if what is seen is a predetermined event. Oftentimes, the conditional dream comes to reveal to us one of four things:

I. Future Blessing or Ministry from the Lord. – The conditional dream reveals to us the things that God has in store for us.

DREAMS AND VISIONS

However, we will not receive the blessing, ministry, etc., except we walk in obedience to the Lord. This is the type of dreams that Joseph had.

> *And Joseph dreamed a dream, and he told it his brethren: and they hated him yet the more. And he said unto them, Hear, I pray you, this dream which I have dreamed: For, Behold, we were binding sheaves in the field, and, lo, my sheaf arose, and also stood upright; and, behold, your sheaves stood round about, and made obeisance to my sheaf. And his*

DREAMS AND VISIONS

brethren said to him, Shalt thou indeed reign over us? Or shalt thou indeed have dominion over us? And they hated him yet the more for his dreams, and for his words. And he dreamed yet another dream, and told it his brethren, and said, Behold, I have dreamed a dream more; and, behold, the sun and the moon and the eleven stars made obeisance to me. (Genesis 37:5-9)

Joseph had two dreams each foretelling of his future leadership and his brother's future submission to him. These dreams were given to him to ensure he would endure the troubled times which were to come. Had Joseph given up during his times of testing, these dreams would not have come to pass. Most dreams involving our future blessings and ministries are conditional. They reveal to us the plan of God, but obedience is always needed to see their fulfillment.

II. Future Blessings and Ministries of Others. – Conditional dreams come to reveal to us the plan of God in the lives of others. Sometimes we will see people receiving blessings, ministering, and in

DREAMS AND VISIONS

other significant life events. God will do this to encourage the other individual to continue in service to Him. God will give these dreams to others to confirm His plan for the individual.

III. Future Spiritual Attacks. – The conditional dream comes to reveal areas of coming spiritual warfare. When this occurs, the person who had the dream and those involved in the dream are called to prayer. This is to ensure that the spiritual attack is averted and handled properly for success.

Since God knows all, He will not allow us to be ignorant of Satan's devices. If these

DREAMS AND VISIONS

dreams are mishandled, individuals will suffer unnecessarily at the hands of the devil's schemes. This form of the conditional dream comes to ensure the success of God's people in spiritual warfare.

IV. Future Unfavorable Events – Contrary to some beliefs, every negative and unfavorable event that occurs is not the result of spiritual warfare. Sometimes, life brings hurt, disappointment, and tragedy. God, in His wisdom, will reveal these things to prompt us to pray for different results.

When these dreams come, sometimes deaths, accidents, job losses, and

DREAMS AND VISIONS

sicknesses are seen. They do not come to scare us but reveal to us what the Lord will do for us if we come to Him in prayer by faith. The conditional dream can be of great blessing if we respond by prayer and obedience.

Regardless of the type of dream that one may have, prayer is to be the foundation for its interpretation and application.

DREAMS AND VISIONS

DREAMS AND VISIONS

Notes:

DREAMS AND VISIONS

- Chapter 4 -
Types of Visions

DREAMS AND VISIONS

DREAMS AND VISIONS

Visions are effective carriers of revelation and insight. However, they can be the source of controversy even among Christians. Many people have used the reception of a "vision" to justify certain courses of action taken.

In addition, some believe that only special individuals can receive visions. Yet, the Lord can speak to whom He wants to in whatever manner He chooses, including visions.

Visions seem to be a higher form of revelation than dreams because they occur usually when one is awake rather than

DREAMS AND VISIONS

asleep (as with dreams). However, visions will accomplish the same tasks as dreams. In this chapter, we will examine the different types of visions and how they are received.

Open Visions

To begin our examination of visions, we will look at the highest manifestation of a vision. Again, the open vision occurs when one is fully awake, and the images are seen with the eyes. There are times when the open vision is seen only by one recipient.

At other times, everyone who is

DREAMS AND VISIONS

present is able to see the vision. Open visions are given at the discretion of the Lord and are used to communicate various messages such as:

I. Call or Commission to Ministry – In both Testaments (especially the Old Testament), God used the open vision to call individuals into ministries. It is still not uncommon for the Lord to do this among His people. Ezekiel received an open vision when the Lord called him and Isaiah also.

Now it came to pass in the thirtieth year, in the fourth month, in the fifth day of the month, as I was among the

DREAMS AND VISIONS

captives by the river of Chebar, that the heavens were opened, and I saw visions of God. (Ezekiel 1:1)

In the year that king Uzziah died I saw also the Lord sitting upon a throne, high and lifted up, and his train filled the temple. (Isaiah 6:1)

II. A Personal or Corporate Prophetic Word – God gives open visions to communicate a prophetic word to an individual or group. This happened frequently to the prophets. The Lord would give them an open vision to communicate

DREAMS AND VISIONS

His prophetic word to them or to His people.

Christians sometimes will receive personal words from the Lord through this type of vision or receive a prophetic word for the Body of Christ. Consider Jeremiah:

> *Moreover, the word of the Lord came unto me, saying, Jeremiah, what seest thou? And I said, I see a rod of an almond tree. Then said the Lord unto me, Thou hast well seen: for I will hasten my word to perform it. And the word of the Lord came unto me the*

DREAMS AND VISIONS

second time, saying, What seest thou? And I said, I see a seething pot; and the face thereof is toward the north. Then the Lord said unto me, Out of the north an evil shall break forth upon all the inhabitants of the land. (Jeremiah 1:11-14)

God used visions to communicate two prophetic messages to Jeremiah which were for His people. The open vision gives a certain authenticity to the prophetic word that accompanies it.

III. Personal Directions and Instructions – Rather than speak to us through the inner

DREAMS AND VISIONS

voice of the Spirit, God will use the open vision to give us directions and instructions in our walk with Him. When God wanted Ananias to go see Saul (later Paul), He used an open vision to give him instructions.

> *And there was a certain disciple at Damascus, named Ananias; and to him said the Lord in a vision, Ananias. And he said, Behold, I am here, Lord. And the Lord said unto him, Arise, and go into the street which is called Straight, and inquire in the house of Judas for one called Saul, of Tarsus:*

DREAMS AND VISIONS

for, behold, he prayeth, And hath seen in a vision a man named Ananias coming in, and putting his hand on him, that he might receive his sight. (Acts 9:10-12)

The scriptures do not say that Ananias was a prophet or held some ministry office, but he was a disciple. However, the Lord chose to use a vision to give him direction. God will still use open visions to communicate to His own.

Though there are other reasons for the open vision, the above three are the most frequently expressed in the scriptures.

DREAMS AND VISIONS

Remember, God will give them to whom He chooses. Now let us consider the next manifestation of a vision; that is, the trance.

Trances

One of the most controversial methods that one receives a vision is that of the trance. Usually trances are associated with cult practices and demonic activity. Yet, the scriptures attest that some of the Lord's servants received visions while they were in trances.

A trance is a state of partly suspended animation or inability to function. In other words, when someone is

DREAMS AND VISIONS

in a trance, he is unable to move or speak. The Spirit of the Lord comes upon them to restrain their movements. It is in this state that the Lord will give them a vision.

Someone may fall into a trance being fully alert while others will experience them when they are about to fall asleep or while they are awakening. We will now look at three examples of God using a trance in the giving of a vision.

When Balaam tried to curse Israel, God stopped him and caused him to bless them. In his final blessing of Israel, the Spirit

DREAMS AND VISIONS

of the Lord came upon him and he fell into a trance seeing a vision.

> *And Balaam lifted up his eyes, and he saw Israel abiding in his tents according to their tribes; and the spirit of God came upon him. And he took up his parable, and said, Balaam the son of Beor hath said, and the man whose eyes are open hath said: He hath said, which heard the words of God, which saw the vision of the Almighty, falling into a TRANCE, but having his eyes open. (Numbers 24:2-4, Emphasis Mine)*

DREAMS AND VISIONS

Before Peter went to preach the Gospel at Cornelius', he fell into a trance where he received a vision. This vision led to the entrance of the Gentiles into the Christian faith.

On the morrow, as they went on their journey, and drew nigh unto the city, Peter went up upon the housetop to pray about the sixth hour: And he became very hungry, and would have eaten: but while they made ready, he fell into a TRANCE, And saw heaven opened, and a certain vessel descending unto him, as it had been a

DREAMS AND VISIONS

great sheet knit at the four corners, and let down to the earth: Wherein were all manner of four-footed beasts of the earth, and wild beasts, and creeping things, and fowls of the air. (Acts 10:9-12, Emphasis Mine)

God could have used any other means, but He chose the trance to reveal His plan to Peter.

When Paul returned to Jerusalem after his conversion, the Lord spoke to him in a trance to leave. He was told that the people would not receive his testimony. He had to leave for his own safety. Again, God

DREAMS AND VISIONS

gave him a vision of these things in a trance.

And it came to pass, that, when I was come again to Jerusalem, even while I prayed in the temple, I was in a TRANCE; And saw him saying unto me, Make haste, and get thee quickly out of Jerusalem: for they will not receive thy testimony concerning me. (Acts 22:17-18, Emphasis Mine)

In the above references, we see three distinct reasons for the trances. The first was to reveal a prophetic word. The second was to reveal God's plan and purpose. The

DREAMS AND VISIONS

third came as warning and direction. God will use trances for many circumstances and situations.

Inner Visions

The most common type of vision among believers is that of the inner vision. An inner vision is a vision that is seen in the mind. It is images given to the mind through the unction of the Spirit of the Lord.

They sometimes appear as quick flashes or images like pictures. At other times, they can be lengthy and full of content.

DREAMS AND VISIONS

Unfortunately, these types of visions are devalued because they are not as dramatic as other types of visions. However, they are to be recognized as valid visions from the Lord and their revelation and content can be trusted.

Some distrust the inner vision because it seems that there is no basis for them in the scriptures. But, this cannot be said with all certainty. There are times when the prophets would say they received a vision, but they did not always say that the visions were open visions.

DREAMS AND VISIONS

We assume that every vision the prophets received were open, this cannot be substantiated. Therefore, it can be concluded that some of the visions they received were inner visions. Consider Elisha and Gehazi:

And Naaman said, Be content, take two talents. And he urged him, and bound two talents of silver in two bags, with two changes of garments, and laid them upon two of his servants; and they bare them before him. And when he came to the tower, he took them from their hand, and

DREAMS AND VISIONS

bestowed them in the house: and he let the men go, and they departed. But he went in, and stood before his master. And Elisha said unto him, Whence comest thou, Gehazi? And he said, Thy servant went no whither. And he said unto him, Went not mine heart with thee, when the man turned again from his chariot to meet thee? Is it a time to receive money, and to receive garments, and oliveyards, and vineyards, and sheep, and oxen, and menservants, and maidservants? (2 Kings 5:23 – 26)

DREAMS AND VISIONS

When Gehazi tried to hide the things that he received from Naaman dishonestly, Elisha asked did not my heart go with you. This demonstrates that he saw what Gehazi did from an inner vision. He made no mention of seeing with his eyes, but with his heart. It was something he saw on the inside. Because of the abiding presence of the Holy Spirit, believers will have inner visions quite often. The Holy Spirit will impress images, pictures, and scenarios in the heart of the believer.

After Paul's conversion, he was blinded. But, when the Lord spoke to

DREAMS AND VISIONS

Ananias to go see Paul, God said that Paul had seen Ananias in a vision coming to him. It was not an open vision because he could not see with his natural eyes. Thus, we understand that he received this vision inwardly.

> *And Saul arose from the earth; and when his eyes were opened, he saw no man: but they led him by the hand, and brought him into Damascus. And he was three days WITHOUT SIGHT, and neither did eat nor drink. And there was a certain disciple at Damascus, named Ananias; and to*

DREAMS AND VISIONS

him said the Lord in a vision, Ananias. And he said, Behold, I am here, Lord. And the Lord said unto him, Arise, and go into the street which is called Straight, and inquire in the house of Judas for one called Saul, of Tarsus: for, behold, he prayeth, And hath SEEN in a VISION a man named Ananias coming in, and putting his hand on him, that he might receive his sight. (Acts 9:8-12, Emphasis Mine)

When one receives an inner vision, it comes unexpectedly. However, it makes an undeniable impression on the recipient. In

DREAMS AND VISIONS

addition, the inner vision is usually accompanied by the word of knowledge to give clarity to what is seen.

Inner visions sometimes come as responses to prayer, ponderings, and questions. Again, inner visions come to accomplish numerous tasks. They can move the believer into a greater understanding of God's plan and purpose even in their individual lives.

Night Visions

The next type of vision after the inner vision is the night vision. Night visions are visions that occur during the night hours.

DREAMS AND VISIONS

Some individuals only experience visions as they are preparing to sleep at night. They cannot fall asleep because the Lord is showing them things in visions. These visions may be open or inner visions. However, they are different from the others because they are received usually during night hours.

These types of visions, like some trances, occur while one is falling asleep or awakening out of sleep. Some individuals who experience these will awake and see a vision then return to sleep. Night visions sometimes occur in succession (one after

DREAMS AND VISIONS

the other) or they are interrupted by moments of sleep and prayerful meditation.

We are introduced to this type of vision in the Book of Daniel. When Daniel asked the Lord for Nebuchadnezzar's dream and its interpretation, God revealed it to him in a night vision.

> *Then was the secret revealed unto Daniel in a night vision. Then Daniel blessed the God of heaven. (Daniel 2:19)*
>
> *After this I saw in the night visions, and behold a fourth beast, dreadful*

DREAMS AND VISIONS

and terrible, and strong exceedingly; and it had great iron teeth: it devoured and brake in pieces and stamped the residue with the feet of it: and it was diverse from all the beasts that were before it; and it had ten horns. (Daniel 7:7)

I saw in the night visions, and, behold, one like the Son of man came with the clouds of heaven, and came to the Ancient of days, and they brought him near before him. (Daniel 7:13)

Some have interpreted Daniel's use of the term night vision to refer to dreams.

DREAMS AND VISIONS

Yet, Daniel had understanding in all dreams and visions.

> *As for these four children, God gave them knowledge and skill in all learning and wisdom: and Daniel had understanding in all visions and dreams. (Daniel 1:17)*

Therefore, if night visions were the same as dreams, he would have called them dreams. In addition, if night visions were not different from other visions, he simply would have called them visions.

It is common for believers to speak of receiving visions while they are trying to go

DREAMS AND VISIONS

to sleep at night. The Lord chooses to reveal things to some during the night. Some think they are dreaming or just seeing things when actually the Lord is giving visions.

Daniel was not the only person who experienced these types of visions. The prophet Zechariah also experienced these types of visions.

...I SAW BY NIGHT, and behold a man riding upon a red horse, and he stood among the myrtle trees that were in the bottom; and behind him were there red horses, speckled, and white.

DREAMS AND VISIONS

(Zechariah 1:7-8, Emphasis Mine)

And the angel that talked with me came again, and waked me, as a man that is wakened out of his sleep. (Zechariah 4:1)

In the above verses, we discover that Zechariah received night visions. In the second reference, Zechariah reports that the angel came and awakened him in order for him to receive the night vision. Night visions come to reveal the plan and purpose of God. God chooses the night when we are at rest and can receive from Him without distraction.

DREAMS AND VISIONS

Visions are still valid expressions of how God communicates even with Christians today.

DREAMS AND VISIONS

DREAMS AND VISIONS

Notes:

DREAMS AND VISIONS

Chapter 5
Other Types of Dreams and Visions

DREAMS AND VISIONS

DREAMS AND VISIONS

Throughout the ages, understanding dreams and visions have troubled many and excited others. We have discussed the types of godly dreams and visions and reasons for their occurrence.

Personal Dreams

Now, we will discuss other types of dreams and visions that are not divinely inspired. These dreams and visions come from other sources and may appear to be vivid and valid as from the Lord, but discernment is needed.

The most difficult of the dreams to interpret and recognize its source is the

DREAMS AND VISIONS

personal dream. A personal dream, simply put, is a dream that comes from within the mind, heart, and soul.

The personal dream is not from the inspiration of the Holy Spirit, nor is it demonically induced. However, it will have the appearance of the other dreams discussed in chapter 3. The difference is that it comes from the thoughts of the heart and the subconscious.

For a dream cometh through the multitude of business; and a fool's voice is known by multitude of words. (Ecclesiastes 5:3)

DREAMS AND VISIONS

The writer of Ecclesiastes states that where there is a lot of activity, dreams will follow. If there are numerous things facing us daily, it is not uncommon to have dreams about these things. These dreams are not coming as warnings or by divine inspiration, but as a way for the mind to sort through activities.

Personal dreams do have certain benefits. They can help us to face our innermost thoughts and fears. Sometimes we will dream about things that we have thought about all day long. Sometimes, if we are in denial with certain things in our

DREAMS AND VISIONS

lives, a personal dream comes to reveal those things to us. Again, personal dreams are caused by things in our hearts and minds based upon:

Activities of the day – If we have various things going on, it will not be uncommon to dream about those things. Even as believers, it will not be uncommon for us to have dreams about being in church or engaging in some religious activity. These things are a part of daily life.

Hidden fears and desires – If we have secret fears and desires, a personal dream may come to reveal it. We may see ourselves

DREAMS AND VISIONS

saying and doing things we would never do in real life. However, the dream comes as a result of these suppressed feelings and emotions.

Secret ambitions – Sometimes when we want something greatly, we may have a dream about doing, receiving, or achieving it. This is where some believers become deceived; especially in areas of ministry.

Someone may dream about preaching, singing, etc. and the Lord has not called him or her to do these things. They may receive it as a prophetic dream, but it is only the desire of their hearts being

DREAMS AND VISIONS

displayed.

> *...neither hearken to your dreams which ye cause to be dreamed. (Jeremiah 29:8b)*

Challenging Situations – If we are faced with tough decisions, sometimes a personal dream will help to clarify our thoughts to make the appropriate decisions. This is one of the beneficial aspects of the personal dream. Personal dreams can be beneficial and deceptive at the same time.

Therefore, as with all dreams, prayerful consideration of them has to be

DREAMS AND VISIONS

done. Do not be afraid of your dreams but ask God for help in understanding their roles in your life.

Demonic Dreams

Continuing our examination, we want to discuss a common weapon against Christians; that is, the demonic dream. As believers, we are consistently in spiritual warfare. The adversary will use any means necessary to distract and frustrate the believer. One way this is done is through demonically induced dreams.

When I say, My bed shall comfort me, my couch shall ease my complaint;

DREAMS AND VISIONS

Then thou scarest me with dreams, and terrifiest me through visions: So that my soul chooseth strangling, and death rather than my life. (Job 7:13-15)

Job said these words when one of his "friends" was trying to use a dream they had to scare him into confessing that he had done wrong. For our study, we find Job's words to be true for how the adversary attacks believers. God promised to bless us and give us peace while we sleep.

I will both lay me down in peace, and

DREAMS AND VISIONS

sleep: for thou, Lord, only makest me dwell in safety. (Psalm 4:8)

It is vain for you to rise up early, to sit up late, to eat the bread of sorrows: for so he giveth his beloved sleep. (Psalm 127:2)

The adversary will come to terrify and distract believers in their dreams. These types of dreams manifest as demonically induced nightmares. Dreams of spirits and wrestling with spirits are common manifestations of the demonic dream.

In addition, dreams of returning to past sins and habits for which one has been

DREAMS AND VISIONS

delivered and has no desire to return are also manifestations of the demonic dream. The demonic dream comes to weaken the believer's resolve to engage in spiritual warfare and walk in holiness. These dreams come oftentimes after spiritual successes, growth, and accomplishments to stop the believer's progress.

False Visions

Concluding our examination of the types of visions, we want to discuss false visions. False visions are visions whose source is not from God or the inspiration of the Holy Spirit. False visions can sometimes

DREAMS AND VISIONS

be hard to detect because they can manifest like other visions. However, their message and content will perform certain things:

Produce Confusion – A false vision will leave the recipient confused as to its meaning and purpose. It will cause individuals to make up its interpretation and its application. If the vision is used to try to minister to someone, the individual will leave confused and frustrated.

> *For God is not the author of confusion... (I Corinthians 14:33a)*

DREAMS AND VISIONS

Produce Fear – False visions will cause individuals to fear what was seen. God does not reveal things to paralyze the believer with fear. A false vision will leave the recipient without hope or understanding of the plan of God.

> *For God hath not given us the spirit of fear; but of power, and of love, and of a sound mind. (II Timothy 1:7)*

Produce Pride – False visions occur sometimes from selfish motives and ambitions. People will have 'visions' of grandeur which will lead to spiritual deception and a fall.

DREAMS AND VISIONS

Pride goeth before destruction, and an haughty spirit before a fall. (Proverbs 16:18)

False visions manifest from three sources. If they are undetected, they will lead to error. The first source of a false vision is *demonic influence*. These visions are demonically induced to breed deception in the recipient and those who will follow the vision.

These types of false visions are generally experienced by occultists, mediums, witches, and the like. Some ordinary people receive these types of false

DREAMS AND VISIONS

visions. They believe if it comes unexpectedly, then it is the Lord.

And no marvel; for Satan himself is transformed into an angel of light. (II Corinthians 11:14)

The devil is a counterfeiter. He will imitate God in order to deceive many. However, believers who are trying to be super-spiritual or looking for great spiritual experiences will set themselves up for this type of false vision.

The second source of a false vision *is human imagination.* Sometimes, individuals can confuse personal desires

DREAMS AND VISIONS

and ambitions with visions from the Lord. In addition, they may confuse fantasies and daydreams with valid visions from the Lord. The false prophets were trapped by this type of false vision. They prophesied, dreamed dreams, and had visions from their own imaginations. They saw what they wanted to see and said it was from the Lord. For these things, they were rebuked.

Then the Lord said unto me, The prophets prophesy lies in my name: I sent them not, neither have I commanded them, neither spake unto them: they prophesy unto you a

DREAMS AND VISIONS

false vision and divination, and a thing of nought, and the deceit of their heart. (Jeremiah 14:14)

As believers, we have to guard against calling our personal desires the visions of the Lord. Because we can see it does not always mean that it is the revelation of the Holy Spirit.

The third source of the false vision is *external influences*. When we are fatigued or under the influence of medications, we can see visions. However, they are the result of physical exhaustion and drug interaction.

DREAMS AND VISIONS

Visions and dreams had during times of great stress and sickness should be handled with extreme caution. Without confirmation and understanding of the Holy Spirit, they should be dismissed without fear. If this is done, when the Lord does give visions, they can be received without hesitation.

Closing Thoughts on Understanding Dreams and Visions

We wanted to conclude our discussion by listing some other facets concerning dreams and visions. These are given to help clarify certain points as we

DREAMS AND VISIONS

endeavor to hear God speak to us through dreams and visions.

- ❖ Not every dream or vision may be from God.
- ❖ Just because you remember the dream and it was full of imagery does not mean it was of the Lord.
- ❖ Dreams in which you have a dream in a dream usually demonstrate that what you see will definitely happen.
- ❖ The most common use of a dream is to provide warning.

DREAMS AND VISIONS

❖ God will never instruct you to do evil from a dream.

In the next book, we will discuss interpreting and applying dreams and visions; understanding the symbols used in dreams and visions; and, the foundation for properly interpreting dreams and visions.

DREAMS AND VISIONS

DREAMS AND VISIONS

Notes:

DREAMS AND VISIONS

www.ingramcontent.com/pod-product-compliance
Lightning Source LLC
Chambersburg PA
CBHW050342010526
44119CB00049B/657